THE FIRST BOOK OF MEZZO-SOPRANO/ALTO SOLOS PART II

compiled by Joan Frey Boytim

G. SCHIRMER, Inc.

DISTRIBUTED BY
HAL•LEONARD®
CORPORATION
7777 W. BLUEMOUND RD. P.O. BOX 13819 MILWAUKEE, WI 53213

PREFACE

The widespread acceptance by teachers and students of "The First Book Series" for Soprano, Mezzo-Soprano/Alto, Tenor, Baritone/Bass has prompted the development of a Part II addition for each voice type. After discussions with numerous voice teachers, the key suggestion expressed many times was that there is a need for "more of the same" type of literature at exactly the same level.

The volumes in Part II follow many of the same concepts which are covered in the Preface of the original volumes, including a comprehensive selection of between 34 and 37 songs from the Baroque through the 20th Century. The selections range from easy to moderate difficulty for both singer and accompanist.

In response to many requests, we have included more sacred songs, and have added two Christmas solos in each volume. The recommendation for more humorous songs for each voice was honored as well.

Even though these books have a heavy concentration of English and American songs, we have also expanded the number of Italian, German, and French offerings. For those using the English singing translations, we have tried to find the translations that are most singable, and in several cases have reworked the texts.

Part II can easily stand alone as a first book for a beginning high school, college, or adult student. Because of the varied contents, Part II can also be successfully used in combination with the first volume of the series for an individual singer. This will give many choices of vocal literature, allowing for individual differences in student personality, maturity, and musical development.

Hal Leonard Publishing (distributor of G. Schirmer) and Richard Walters, supervising editor, have been most generous in allowing the initial objective for this series to be expanded more fully through publishing these companion volumes. We hope this new set of books will provide yet another interesting and exciting new source of repertoire for both the teacher and student.

Joan Frey Boytim
September, 1993

About the Compiler...

Since 1968, Joan Frey Boytim has owned and operated a full-time voice studio in Carlisle, Pennsylvania, where she has specialized in developing a serious and comprehensive curriculum and approach to teaching and coaching adolescent and community adult students. Her teaching experience has also included music and choral instruction at the junior high and senior high levels, and voice instruction at the college level. She is the author of a widely used bibliography, *Solo Vocal Repertoire for Young Singers* (a publication of NATS), and, as a nationally recognized expert on teaching beginning vocal study, has been featured in many speaking engagements and presentations on the subject.

CONTENTS

AH! MIO COR

(Ah! my heart)

English by Theodore Baker

George Frideric Handel

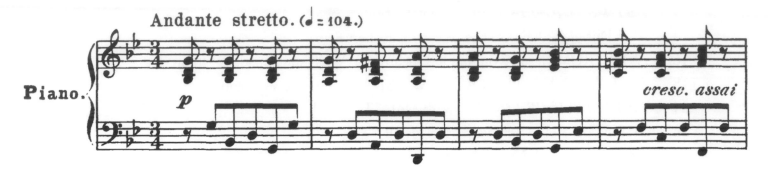

Ah!____ mio cor,
Ah,____ poor heart!

Printed in the USA by G. Schirmer, Inc.

Tempo I.

scher - ni - to   se - i.
he   scorns thy   love.

Stel - le,   De - i,   Nu - me d'a - mo - re!   tra - di -
Hear me,   Heaven,   ye gods a - bove!   Thee, O

to - re,   t'a - mo tan - to,   puoi la - sciar - mi sola in
trai - tor,   love I on - ly,   Canst thou leave me weeping

pian - to?   Oh   De - i!   puoi la - sciar - mi, oh
lone - ly?   O   Heaven!   canst thou   leave me,   O

6

De - i, per - chè? t'a - mo tan - to,
Heav - en! and why? So I love thee,

puo - i la - sciar - mi so - la, so - la,
canst_____ thou leave me weeping, weeping,

so - la in pian - to, puoi la - sciar - mi, oh De - i, per -
weeping and lone - ly, canst thou leave me, O Heav-en! and

chè?
why?

7

8

AS I WENT A-ROAMING

Helen Taylor

May H. Brahe

Printed in the USA by G. Schirmer, Inc.

He_ said, "You shall walk in a gown made of_ rall. sat_in, A ring on your fin_ger, a rose at your ear; And you shall ride forth in a coach with six_ hor_ses, And I'll love you tru_ly, if you'll be my dear. Der_ry der_ry down der_ry oh!

Der_ry der_ry down der_ry oh! Der_ry down der_ry, if you'll be my
dear." Then he gave me a kiss, and I could not re_strain him, His
words were so sweet and so pleas_ing to hear; And_ so I will
wed him with_out more de_lay_ing, Since he is my true love and

Tempo Iº
Very brightly.

I am his dear. Der_ry der_ry down der_ry oh!

Der_ry der_ry down der_ry oh! Der_ry down der_ry oh! I am his

poco rall. *un poco accel.*

dear, oh!— Der_ry der_ry down der_ry oh! Der_ry der_ry down

poco rall. *un poco accel.*

rall.

der_ry oh! Der_ry down der_ry oh!— I am his dear.

rall.

sf sf

AUF DEM MEERE

(On the Ocean)

Heinrich Heine
English by Henry G. Chapman

Robert Franz
Op. 36, No 1.
Original key E major.

AVE VERUM

(Jesu, Word of God Incarnate)

Wolfgang Amadeus Mozart

Printed in the USA by G. Schirmer, Inc.

BENEATH A WEEPING WILLOW'S SHADE

Francis Hopkinson
arranged by
Harold Milligan

Be - neath a weep - ing wil - low's shade, She
E - cho to ____ her strains ___ re - plied, The

sat and sang ___ a - lone, _____ Be - neath ___ a weep - ing
winds her sor - rows bore, _____ Fond E - cho to ___ her

Printed in the USA by G. Schirmer, Inc.

wil - low's shade,__ She sat__ and sang__ a - lone;__ Her
strains__ re - plied,__ The winds__ her sor - rows bore;__ "A -

poco rit.   *mf*

poco rit.

hand up - on__ her heart__ she laid, And plain - tive was__ her
dieu dear youth,__ A - dieu!__ she cried, "I ne'er shall see__ thee

poco rit.

p a tempo

moan,_____ And plain - tive was__ her moan._____ The__
more,_____ I ne'er__ shall see__ thee more."_____

p a tempo

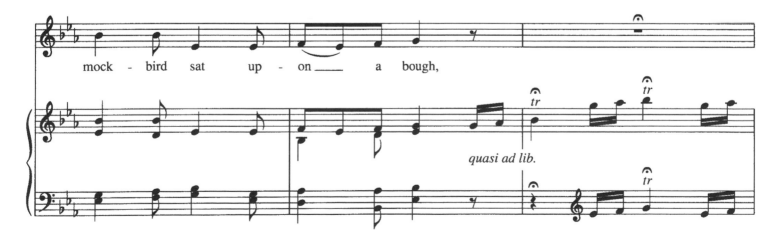

mock - bird sat up - on__ a bough,

tr *tr*

quasi ad lib.

tr

way_____ the dul - cet notes a - way_____ the

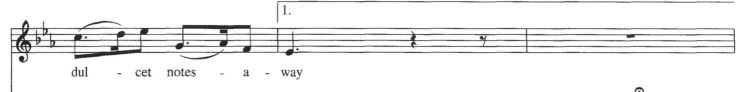

1.

dul - cet notes - a - way

quasi ad lib.

rit.   a tempo

Fond

2.

way.

THE BLUE-BELL

from "An Old Garden"

Verse by
Margaret Deland

Edward MacDowell

BIST DU BEI MIR

(You Are With Me)

Anonymous
translation by Hansel Powell

J. S. Bach

Bist du bei mir, geh' ich mit Freu - den
You are with me, my joy for - ev - er.

zum Ster - ben____ und zu mei - ner____ Ruh', zum_____ Ster - ben und zu mei - ner
Un - til____ my____ death and un - to my rest, un - til my death and un - to

Ruh'. Bist du____ bei____ mir, geh' ich mit
rest. You are____ with____ me, my joy for

THE CAROL OF THE BIRDS

text by the composer

John Jacob Niles

Christ - mas day in the morn - ing, cu - roo, cu-roo, cu - roo, _____ cu-

roo, cu - roo, _ cu - roo. _____ The lark, the dove, the red - bird came, cu-

roo, cu - roo, cu - roo, _____ The lark, the dove, the red - bird came And

wor-shipped there in Je - sus' name, On Christ-mas day in the morn - ing, cu -

roo, cu - roo, cu - roo, _____ cu - roo, cu - roo, _ cu - roo. _____

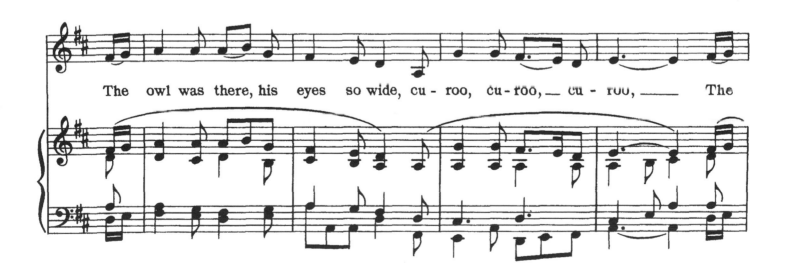

The owl was there, his eyes so wide, cu - roo, cu-roo, _ cu - roo, _____ The

owl was there, his eyes so wide As he did sit at sweet Ma-ry's side On

Christ-mas day in the morn - ing, cu - roo, cu-roo, cu - roo, _____ cu-

roo, cu - roo, cu - roo. _____ The shep-herd knelt up - on the hay, cu-

roo, cu - roo, — cu - roo, — The shep - herd knelt up - on the hay, As

an - gels sang the night a-way And God pro-claim-ed the ho - ly day, cu-

roo, cu-roo, cu - roo, — cu - roo, cu - roo, cu - roo. —

CARMEÑA

Ellis Walton

H. Lane Wilson

Ah! _____ come, ah, come!

Ah! _____ Love, I watch _____ the scene _____ so

bright. _____ Ah! now_rings a voice I know from ev-'ry

voice a - part,_____Thro'the o - range grove he hastens, He is coming, oh, my

34

heart!_____ Ah! now rings a voice I know from ev-'ry voice a-

part,____ Thro' the o - range grove he hast-ens,__ He is coming, oh, my

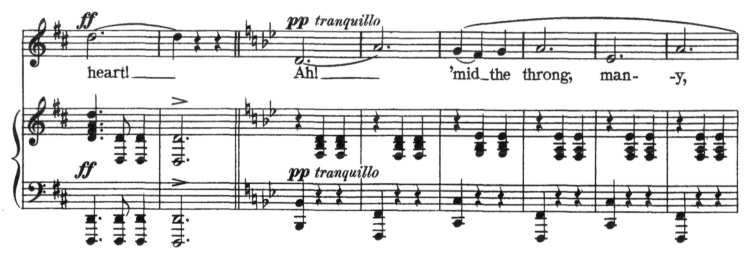

heart!____ Ah!____ 'mid the throng, man- -y,

many are fair; Bright____ flow-'rets twine in ra - ven .

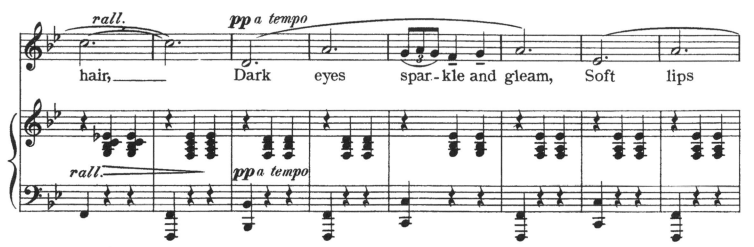

C'EST MON AMI

(My Friend)

translation by Alice Mattullath

Old French Air
arranged by Bainbridge Crist

39

know-ing him your love grows fond - er, Bring him to me,
aime en - sui - te da - van - ta - ge: C'est mon a - mi,

lov - ers are we! I have his heart and mine has he;
ren - dez - le moi! J'ai son a - mour, il a ma foi;

I have his heart and mine has he.____
J'ai son a - mour, il a ma foi.____

If he can wake the ech - oes sleep - ing With - in the
Si, par sa voix ten - dre et plain - ti - ve, Il char -

woods as he goes by, And if his flute's sweet
me l'é - cho _ de vos bois; Si les ac - cents _ de

mel - o - dy Can move the shep-herd-ess to weep - -
son haut - bois Ren-dent la ber - gè - - re pen - si - -

ing, Bring him to me, lov - ers are we!
ve, C'est en - cor lui, ren - dez - le moi!

riten.   *a tempo*

I have his heart and mine has he, I have his
J'ai son a - mour, il a ma foi, J'ai son a -

riten.   *a tempo*

heart and mine has he. ___
mour, il a ma foi. ___

If to some poor and need-y ___
Si pas - sant près de sa chau-miè-

broth - er, Who is not young and strong of limb, And
re Le pauvre, en voy - ant son trou - peau,

came to ask a lamb of him, He'd give the
O__ se de-man-der un a - - gneau Et qu'il ob -

lamb-kin and its moth - - er, Mine he must be,
tienne en-cor la mè - - re. Oh! c'est bien lui,

riten.   *a tempo*

lov - ers are we! I have his heart and mine has
ren-dez-le moi! J'ai son a - mour, il a ma

riten.   *a tempo*

rit.

he, I__ have his heart and mine has he.
foi, J'ai son a - mour, il a ma foi.__

rit.

$\mathit{Ped.}$ *pp*

CLOUDS

Author unknown

Ernest Charles

One lit-tle hour we know their grace— They pass like shad-ows, nor hold their

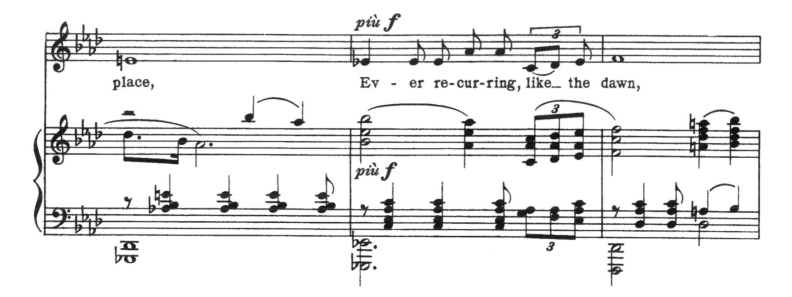

place, Ev - er re-cur-ring, like the dawn,

Nev-er en-dur-ing, but al-ways gone, Part of the in-fi-nite, shall we say,

Part of the mo-ment we call to - day.

Clouds a-drift in the sum-mer sky

Re-sem-ble Life, as they wan - der by.

COME YE BLESSED

from *The Holy City*

Matthew 25:34

Alfred Gaul

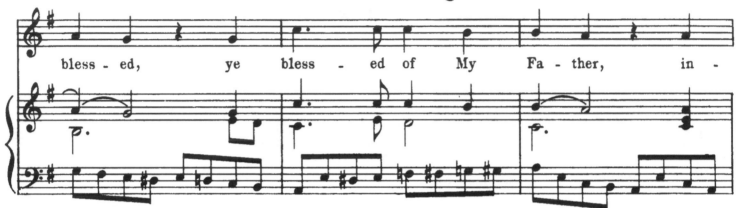

Printed in the USA by G. Schirmer, Inc.

48

give, to give you the king-dom, the king - dom pre -

par'd, pre - par'd for you, come,

come, come, come,

Come, ye bless - ed, ye bless - ed of my

Fa - ther, in - her - it the king - dom, the king-dom prepar'd for you, come, ye blessed, come, ye bless - ed, in - her - it the kingdom pre- par'd for you from the foun - da - tion of the world

rit.

colla voce.

colla voce.

a tempo.
legato.

rall.

CRÉPUSCULE
(Twilight)

Armand Silvestre
English version by
Lorraine Noel Finley

Jules Massenet

52

es. _____ Les lys ne dor - ment qu'un mo - ment
ing. _____ The lil - ies' sleep is__ quick-ly past.

ppp

Veux - tu pas que tê - tes pen - ché - es, Nous cau-sions
With heads in-clined and vig - il keep - - ing, Shall we not

ritard. *poco a*

a - mou-reu-se-ment, Nous cau-sions a - mou-reu-se-ment? Les coc-ci-
talk of love at last, Shall we not talk of love at last While lit - tle

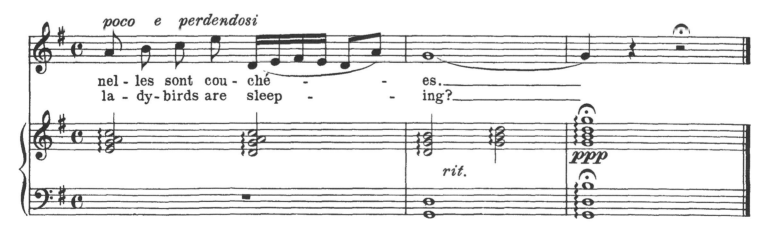

poco e perdendosi

nel - les sont cou - ché - - es._____
la - dy-birds are sleep - - ing?_____

rit. *ppp*

DANNY BOY

Fred E. Weatherly

Old Irish Air

Oh, Dan-ny Boy, the pipes, the pipes are call - ing.......... From glen to glen, and down the moun - tain side,........................... The sum - mer's

But when ye come, and all the flow'rs are dy - ing,......... If I am dead, as dead I well may be,......... Ye'll come and find the place where I am

ly - ing,......... And kneel and say an A - ve there for me;......... And I shall

hear,   though soft you tread a - bove.... me,......... And all my

grave will warm-er, sweet-er be,.......................... For you will

sempre pp   *poco rit.*

bend   and tell me that you   love...... me,............. And I shall

più lento.   *rall.*

sleep in peace un - til you come to   me!..

DREAM VALLEY

William Blake

Roger Quilter

ELÉGIE

Louis Gallet
translation by Alice Mattullath

Jules Massenet

Triste et très lent
Sadly and slowly

très expressif avec accablement
very expressive and dejected

Voice

Piano

Ô ___ doux prin - temps d'au - tre - fois,
O ___ Spring of days long gone by,

rit.

expressif et soutenu
expressive and sustained

Ver - tes sai - sons,
where is thy bloom?

Vous a - vez fui pour tou - jours!___
Blos - soms no long - er I see!___

Je ne vois
I see no

imitez le chant
espress.

plus le ciel bleu;
blue in the sky,

Je n'en-tends plus
I hear no song,

les chants joy-eux des oi-
birds do not car - rol to

seaux!
me!

En em - por - tant mon bon heur,___
All that I cherish-ed has flown,___

Ô
Love,

bien - ai-
since you

cresc.

cresc. ed animato poco

Printed in the USA by G. Schirmer, Inc.

DAS ERSTE VEILCHEN

(The First Violet)

from *Egon Erbert*
by W. Bartholomew

Felix Mendelssohn

When I be -
Als ich das

held the first vio - let bloom, I gaz'd on its
er - - ste Veil - chen er - blickt, wie war ich von

beau - ty, I breath'd its per - fume; The her - ald of
Far - ben und Duft ent - zückt! Die Bo - tin des

64

breast.
Brust.

a tempo.

The Spring is de-part-ed, the vio-let is dead,_____
Der Lenz ist vor-ü-ber, das Veil-chen ist tot,_____

the vio-let is dead! Flow-ers more gay now deck its
das Veil-chen ist tot; rings stehn viel Blu-men, blau und

bed. Un-heed-ed they blossom, in mem'ry I see The vio-let, the
rot, ich ste-he in-mit-ten, und se-he sie kaum, ich ste-he in-

vio-let, in mem'..ry I see _____ The vio -
mit-ten, und se - he sie kaum, _____ das Veil- -

- let, the vio - let that first bloom'd so sweet-ly for me, The
- chen, das Veil - chen er - scheint mir im Früh - lings - traum, das

vio - - - let that first bloom'd, that first bloom'd so
Veil - - - chen er - scheint mir, er - scheint mir im

sweetly for me.
Frühlingstraum

ES MUSS EIN WUNDERBARES SEIN

(It Must Be Wonderful)

Oscar von Redwitz

Franz Liszt

Printed in the USA by G. Schirmer, Inc.

so mit ein - an - der tra - gen, so mit ein -
Is shared be - tween them whol - ly, Is shared be -

an - der tra - gen, vom ers - ten Kuss bis in den
tween them whol - ly; For all their life till death shall

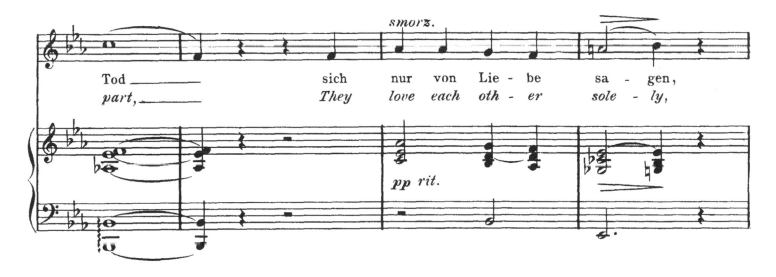

Tod _____ sich nur von Lie - be sa - gen,
part, _____ They love each oth - er sole - ly,

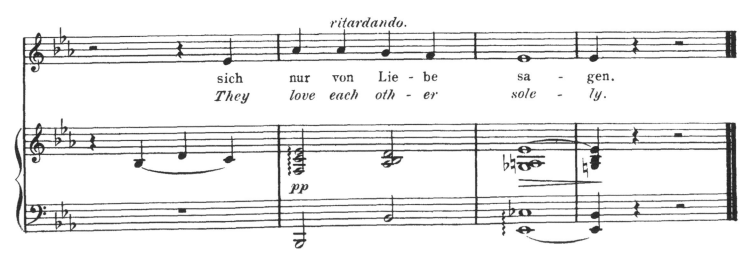

sich nur von Lie - be sa - gen.
They love each oth - er sole - ly.

GOTT IM FRÜHLING

(God in Springtime)

J. P. Uz
translation by Lorraine Noel Finley

Franz Schubert

Stun - den, o Gott, auf sei - nen Blu - men -
clos - es, O Lord, her love-ly throne of

thron. Er geht in Bü - schen, und sie
flow'rs. The spring makes bush - es burst in

blühn; den Flu - ren kommt ihr fri - sches Grün, und
bloom, While mead - ows ear - ly green as-sume, And

Wäl - dern wächst ihr Schatten wie - der, der
shade to wood - land is re - stor - ing. The

West, lieb - ko - send, schwingt sein tau - en - des Ge -
gen - tle West Wind stirred Its dew - y feath - ers

fie - der, und je - der fro - he Vo - gel singt. Mit
soar - ing, And ev - 'ry hap - py bird is heard. To

(colla voce) (a tempo) mf

eu - rer Lie - der süs - sem Klang, ihr Vö - gel,
join your car - ols in the skies, O birds, my

mf

soll auch mein Ge - sang zum Va - ter
song shall al - so rise To God who

più f

cresc.

der Na - tur sich schwin - gen. Ent - zü - ckung reisst mich
made all crea - tures liv - ing. My joy is ver - y

with exaltation

hin, ich will dem Herrn lob - sin - gen, durch
great: To Him I sing thanks - giv - ing Through

slight retard

den ich wur - de was ich bin!
whom I reach this hap - py state!

colla voce　*a tempo*

quietly to the end

KEINE SORG' UM DEN WEG

(Love Finds Out the Way)

J. Raff

seh'n woll'n, ___ wie bald ist's ge-macht! Da giebt's einen Mondschein,
meet - ing, ___ Love lends them a light! Moonlight will shine for them,

da scheint wohl ein Stern, da blinkt noch ein Licht-lein, man nimmt ei-ne La-
stars sil-ver-rayed Brightly will twin-kle to give them their

tern'; da fin-det sich schon ei-ne Lei-ter, ein Steg, ___ ein Steg, ___
aid? Nothing can daunt them by night or by day, ___ by day, ___

___ wenn zwei sich nur gut sind, ___ kei-ne Sorg' um den Weg, wenn
___ If two are true lov-ers, ___ Love will find out a way, If

zwei sich nur gut sind, ___ kei-ne Sorg' um den Weg. ___
two are true lov-ers, ___ Love will find out a way. ___

A LEGEND

Pleshtchéyeff
translated by Nathan Haskell Dole

Pytor Il'yichTchaikovsy

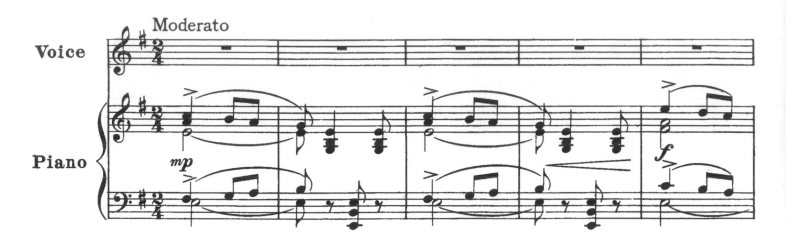

Christ, when a child, a gar - den
L'en - fant Jé - sus dans son jar -

made, And man - y ros - es flour - ished there,
din A - vait plan - té de bel - les roses.

Printed in the USA by G. Schirmer, Inc.

76

THE LOVELY SONG MY HEART IS SINGING

text by the composer

Edmund Goulding

drift - ing down on beams of moon - light, To

rest with - in our mo - ment, my be - lov - ed, When

I'm a - lone, it's soft and plead - ing, When

you   are here my whole world rings!_____ The

ech - o of that mo-ment al - ways brings the

love - ly song that my heart sings._____

MYSTERY'S SONG

from *The Fairy Queen*

E. Settle
after *A Midsummer Night's Dream*
by William Shakespeare

Henry Purcell

Original Key C mi.

Printed in the USA by G. Schirmer, Inc.

'Tis ho - ly, 'tis ho - ly and we must, we—

must— con - ceal it; They— pro - fane— it,

they— pro - fane— it— who— re - veal it,

They pro - fane it, they pro - fane it— who— re - veal it.

MARIÄ WIEGENLIED
(The Virgin's Slumber Song)

Martin Boelitz
English version by Edward Teschemacher

Max Reger

Amid the ros-es Ma-ry sits and
Ma - ri - a sitzt am Ro - sen-hag und

rocks her Je-sus-child, While a-mid the tree-tops
wiegt ihr Je - sus-kind, durch die Blät - ter lei - se

sighs the breeze so warm and mild.
weht der war - me Som - mer - wind.

And soft and sweet-ly sings a bird up-on a bough:
Zu ihr - en Fü - ssen singt ein bun - tes Vö - ge-lein:

Ah, ba - by, dear_____ one,
Schlaf', Kind - lein, sü - - - - sse,

rit. - - - - -
dolciss.

slum - - - ber now!
schlaf'_____ nun ein!

Hap - py is Thy laugh - ter, ho - ly is__ Thy
Hold__ ist dein Lä - cheln, hol - der dei - nes

NYMPHS AND SHEPHERDS

Thomas Shadwell

Henry Purcell

this,   this is   Flo - ra's   ho - ly - day,   this   is

Flo - ra's   ho - ly - day,   this   is   Flo - ra's   ho - ly -

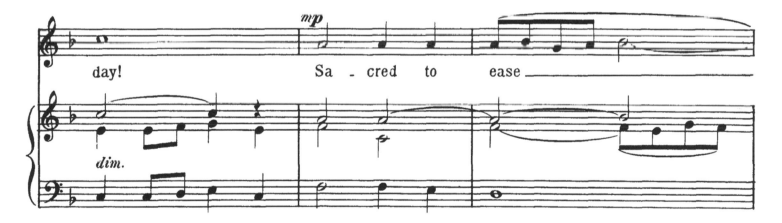

day!   Sa - cred   to   ease

and   hap - py   love,   To

dan_cing, to mu _ _ _ _ sic, to danc_ing, to

leggiero

cresc.

mu _ _ _ _ _ _ _ sic and to po _ et _ ry.

dim.

l.h.

p dolce

mf

dim.

Your flock may now, now, now, now, now, now, now, now, now,

dim.

tranquillo

cresc.

molto cresc.

now, se _ cure _ ly_ rove;_ Whilst you ex _ press, whilst

mf leggiero

you ex - press _____ your

slarg. e dolce

jol - i - try! Nymphs and shepherds,

marcato il basso

p slarg:

cresc.

come _ a - way, come a - way, Nymphs and shep _ herds,

p

cresc.

rit.

come _ a - way, come a - way, come, come, come, _ come _ a - way!

colla voce

REND'IL SERENO AL CIGLIO
(Bring to Your Eyes)
from *Sosarme*

English version by Joan Boytim

George Frideric Handel

Largo (Very slowly)

Rend' il se - re - no al ci - glio, ma - dre, non pian - ger
Bring to your eyes re - newed calm - ness, moth - er, now weep no

più, non pian - ger più, nò. ma - dre, non pian - ger___
more, now weep no more. No! Moth - er, now weep no___

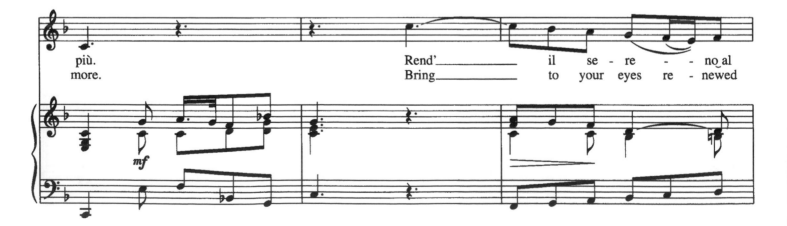

più. Rend'_____ il se - re - no al
more. Bring_____ to your eyes re - newed

Printed in the USA by G. Schirmer, Inc.

93

ci - glio
calm - ness.

ma - dre, non pian - ger più,
Moth - er, now weep no more.

nò
No,

nò ma - dre, non pian - ger
no, moth - er, now weep no

più.
more.

Te - mer d'al - cun pe -
For - get all thoughts of

Rend'_____ il se - re - -no al ci - glio
Bring_____ to your eyes re - newed calm - ness.

ma - dre, non pian - ger__ più, nò
Moth - er, now weep no__ more. No!

nò ma - dre, non__ pian - ger più.
No! Moth - er, now weep no more.

cresc. *f* *p* *f* *p* *f*

3

SEPARAZIONE
(Parting)

English version by
Henry G. Chapman

Italian Folksong
arranged by
Giovanni Sgambati

Lentamente
Con accento passionale

Do - - lo - ro - - sa par -
Full of sad - - ness this

ten - za, ahi!__ quan - - to è du - - ra!
part-ing: Ah, how hard_____ so to leave_____ thee!

Quanto è gran - de per me__ la pe - na, la pe - na a - ma -
Oh, how sore__ is the pain, the__ sor - row, the sor - row it__ gives__

rall.

Printed in the USA by G. Schirmer, Inc.

SÉRÉNADE
(Sing, Smile, Slumber)

Victor Hugo
English version by Willis Wager

Charles Gounod
edited by Carl Deis

1. Quand tu chan-tes ber-cé-e Le soir en-tre mes bras,
2. Quand tu ris, sur ta bou-che L'a-mour s'é-pa-nou-it;
1. When you sing while I hold you At eve close in my arms,
2. When you smile in your laugh-ter Fair love bursts in-to bloom;

100

tez, chan-tez____ tou - jours,____ Chan - tez,_____ chan-tez, ma
ez, ri - ez____ tou - jours,____ Ri - ez,_____ ri - ez, ma
on, sing on____ for aye,____ Sing on,_____ sing on, en -
on, smile on____ for aye,____ Smile on,_____ smile on, thou

bel - le, Chan-tez tou - jours! Chan - tez, ma____ bel - le, Chan -
bel - le, Ri˙- ez tou - jours! Ri - ez, ma____ bel - le, Ri -
thrall-ing, Sing on for aye, Sing____ on, en - thrall-ing, Sing____
charm-ing, Smile on for aye, Smile____ on, thou____ charm-ing, Smile____

tez____ tou - jours!_____
ez____ tou - jours!_____
on____ for____ aye._____
on____ for____ aye._____

102

mez, dor - mez,__ ma bel - le, Dor - mez, dor - mez__ tou - jours,__ Dor -
on, dream on,__ so ten - der, Dream on, dream on__ for aye,__ Dream

mez,_____ dor - mez, ma bel - le, Dor - mez tou - jours! Dor -
on,_____ dream on, so ten-der, Dream on for__ aye,__ Dream__

mez, ma__ bel - le, Dor - mez,__ dor - mez__ tou -
on,__ so ten - der, Dream on,__ dream__ on__ for__

jours!_____
aye._____

THE SLEEP THAT FLITS ON BABY'S EYES

Rabindranath Tagore

John Alden Carpenter

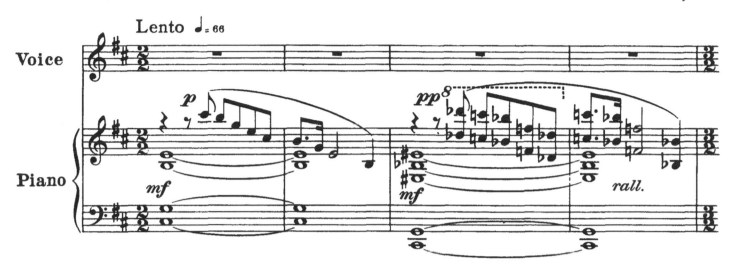

The sleep that flits __ on ba - by's eyes, does an-y-bod-y

know __ from where it comes?

Printed in the USA by G. Schirmer, Inc.

Ancora più mosso ♩ = 112

Yes, there is a ru-mour that it has its dwell-ing where, in the

fair - y vil-lage a-mong the shad-ows of the for - est

il basso sempre p

dim - ly lit with glow - worms,

rall.

p

pp

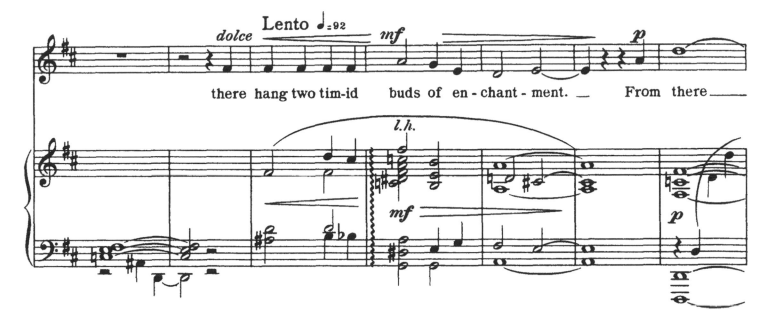

there hang two tim-id buds of en-chant-ment. _ From there___

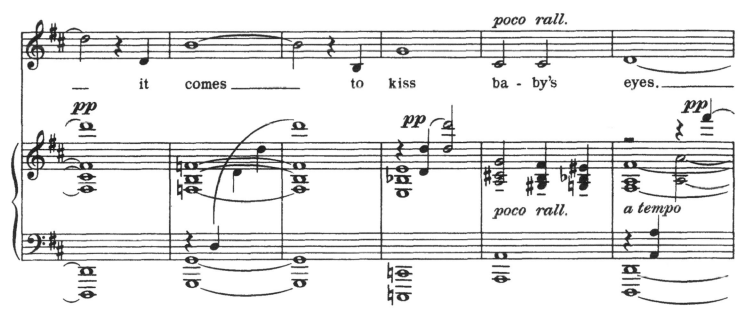

_ it comes ____ to kiss ba - by's eyes.__

SPRING IS AT THE DOOR

Nora Hopper

Roger Quilter

ro - sy feet are bare, The wind is in her hair, And

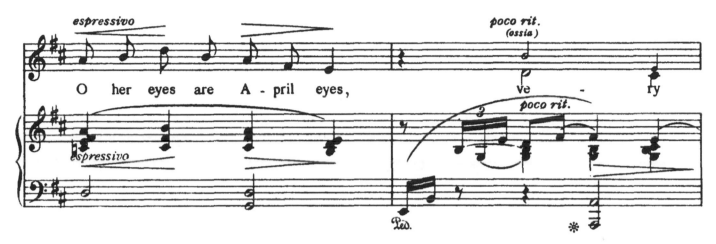

O her eyes are A - pril eyes, ve - ry

fair. Af - ter her foot-steps fol - low The

mul - lein and the mal - low; She scat - ters gold - en pow - der on the

108

sal - low. She brings the cro - cus white, And gold - en

ac - o - nite: She brings de - sire and doubt - ing and de -

- light. The

Spring is at the door: She bears a gold - en store, Her

maund with yel - low daf - fo - dils run - neth o'er._____ Her

ro - sy feet are bare, The wind is in her hair, And

espressivo *poco rit.*

O her eyes are A - pril eyes, ve - ry

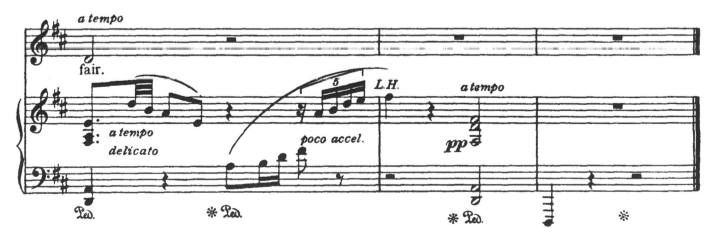

a tempo

fair.

DIE STILLE

(Silence)

Joseph, Freiherr von Eichendorff
translation by Theodore Baker

Robert Schumann

Es weiss und räth es doch Kei-ner, wie mir so wohl ist, so wohl! Ach
There's none can know it or feel it, How all my heart is a-glow! Ah,

wüsst' es nur Ei-ner, nur Ei-ner, kein Mensch es sonst wis-sen sollt'. So
on - ly to one would I tell it, And no-bod-y else should know. So

still ist's nicht draussen im Schnee, so stumm und ver-schwiegen sind die
si-lent the snow does not lie, So mute and so qui - et are Not

Ster - ne nicht in der Höh', als mei - ne Ge-dan-ken sind.___ Ich
e'en the stars in the sky As the thoughts that I'm thinking are.___ I

Printed in the USA by G. Schirmer, Inc.

DIE STILLE WASSERROSE

(The Silent Waterlily)

E. Giebel
Translation by Theodore Baker

Alexander von Fielitz

an. _____ Er singt so süss, so lei - se, und will im Singen ver-
on. _____ He sings so sweet, so fond - ly, In song his life would ex-

geh'n; _____ o Blu - me, wei - sse Blu - me, kannst du das Lied_ ver-
hale; _____ Oh flow - er, snow - y flow - er, Canst thou his mean - ing

stehn? _____
tell? _____

WEEP NO MORE

from *Hercules*

John Fletcher

George Frideric Handel

Printed in the USA by G. Schirmer, Inc.

Vio - lets plucked, the sweet - est rain Makes not fresh nor

grow a - gain, nor grow a - gain.

Joys as wing - ed dreams fly fast, Why should

sad - ness, why should sad - ness long - er last? Joys as

TE DEUM
(Vouchsafe, O Lord)

English version by
R. L. Beckhard

George Frideric Handel

nos - tri Do-mi-ne,   mi - se - re - re.   Fi - at mi-se - ri-
Lord, __ be mer-ci-ful,   Lord,   have mer-cy.   Lord, let Thy mer - cy

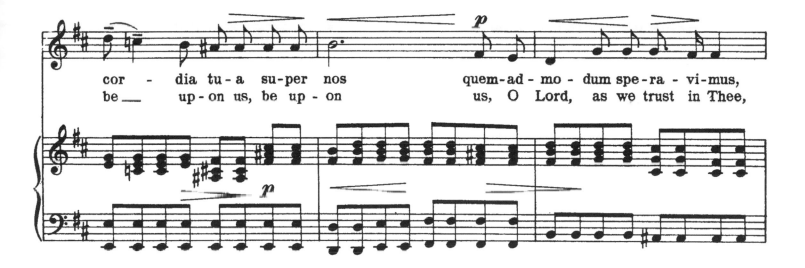

cor - dia tu-a su-per nos   quem-ad-mo-dum spe-ra - vi-mus,
be __ up-on us, be up-on   us, O Lord,   as we trust in Thee,

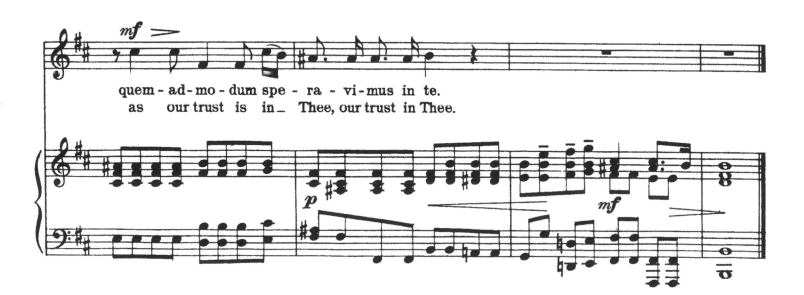

quem - ad-mo-dum spe-ra - vi-mus in te.
as   our trust is in_ Thee, our trust in Thee.

WHEN I HAVE OFTEN HEARD
YOUNG MAIDS COMPLAINING
from *The Fairy Queen*

E. Settle
after *A Midsummer Night's Dream*
by William Shakespeare

Henry Purcell

Original Key C

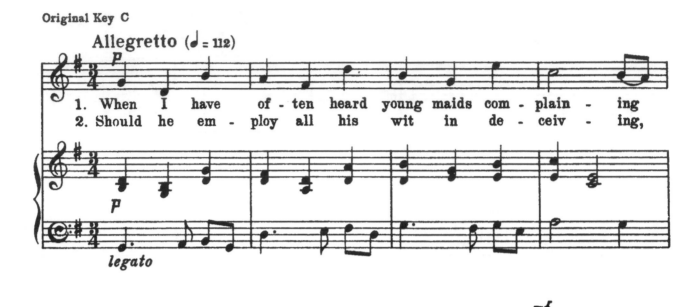

1. When I have of-ten heard young maids com-plain - ing
2. Should he em - ploy all his wit in de - ceiv - ing,

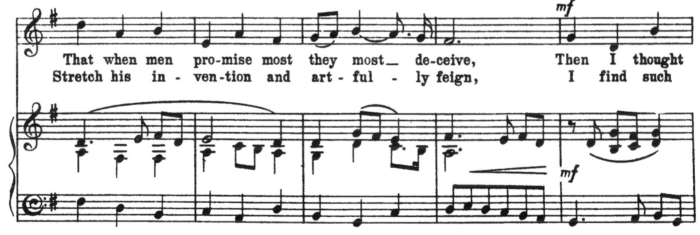

That when men pro-mise most they most__ de-ceive, Then I thought
Stretch his in - ven-tion and art - ful - ly feign, I find such

none of them wor - thy my gain - ing, And what they
charms, such true joy in be - liev - ing, I'll have the

Printed in the USA by G. Schirmer, Inc.

swore re-solv'd ne'er to be-lieve. But when so hum-bly he
plea-sure, let him have the pain. If he proves per-jur'd, I

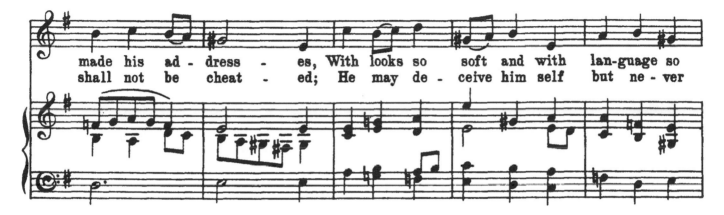

made his ad-dress-es, With looks so soft and with lan-guage so
shall not be cheat-ed; He may de-ceive him self but ne-ver

kind, I thought it sin to re-fuse his came: 'Tis what I look for and shan't be de-

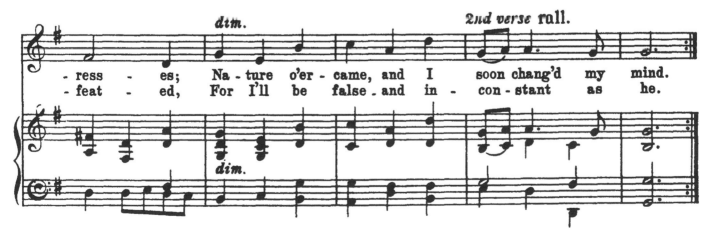

-ress-es; Na-ture o'er-came, and I soon chang'd my mind.
-feat-ed, For I'll be false and in-con-stant as he.

THE WILLOW SONG

from *Othello*
by William Shakespeare

Arthur Sullivan

The poor soul sat sigh - ing by a syc - a - more tree, Sing

all___ a green wil - low; Her hand on her bo - som, her

Printed in the USA by G. Schirmer, Inc.

wil - low, wil - low, wil - low, _____ Sing

all a green wil - low must be _____ my gar - land, Sing

wil - low, wil - low, wil - low.

The fresh streams ran by her, and

WIND OF THE WHEAT

Harold Simpson

Montague F. Phillips

Allegretto grazioso. ♩ = 144.

The

wind runs o'er the wheat On fai-ry feet, _____

A little slower.

_____ And to the wav-ing corn _____ It whis - pers in the

wind   runs o'er   the   wheat   On fai-ry feet,____

____ The pop-pies all are blown― And I   am here'a-lone, And I am

here_____ a - lone!_____